HOW TO GET THE PERFECT BODY

HOW TO GET THE PERFECT BODY

Book design copyright@2020 ProtectMyWork.com

Visit the author's website at www.leangains.co.uk

Published in United Kingdom

ISBN: 978-1-9163812-0-9 (Paperback)

CONTENTS

SO, WHO AM I??

...AND MORE IMPORTANTLY, WHY SHOULD YOU LISTEN TO WHAT I HAVE TO SAY????....

DR JONATHAN S. LEE

"I AM A QUALIFIED SPORTS NUTRITIONIST AND PERSONAL TRAINER WHO HAS SUCCESSFULLY WORKED WITH THOUSANDS OF CLIENTS OVER THE PAST 20 YEARS."

"I ATTAINED MY BACHELOR OF SCIENCE IN NUTRITION AND MEDICAL SCIENCE AFTER ATTENDING KING'S COLLEGE LONDON IN 1998."

"IN ADDITION, I'VE SPENT THE LAST 8 YEARS OF MY LIFE RESEARCHING THE SCIENCE BEHIND FAT LOSS, MUSCLE GROWTH, HEALTHY LIVING, ANTI-AGEING, AND OVERALL WELL-BEING."

"SO FAR, I HAVE WRITTEN A TOTAL OF 6 BOOKS ALL SPECIALISING IN VARIOUS ASPECTS OF HEALTH AND FITNESS, EXERCISE, AND WEIGHT TRAINING."

"IN MY EARLY TWENTIES, I WAS CLINICALLY OBESE WITH A BODY FAT PERCENTAGE OF 28!!! AFTER JOINING ALL THE DOTS AND PUTTING ALL THE PIECES TOGETHER, I WAS ABLE TO SUCCESSFULLY LOSE 18% BODY FAT IN 10 MONTHS AND ABOVE ALL KEEP THE WEIGHT OFF FOR GOOD!!

...SO WHAT WILL YOU GET FROM READING THIS BOOK??...

LET'S GET TO THE POINT!!! THIS BOOK CONTAINS TRIED-AND-TESTED, SCIENCE-BACKED FORMULAS AND ADVICE THAT YOU WILL NOT FIND IN THE MAJORITY OF FITNESS BOOKS OUT THERE!!
(TRUST ME, I'VE READ LOADS OF FITNESS BOOKS!!)

BY THE WAY, I'LL TELL YOU NOW THAT THIS BOOK DOES NOT CONTAIN ANY WORKOUT ROUTINES AND THIS IS INTENTIONAL!! I'VE WRITTEN 2 SEPARATE BOOKS FOR THAT:

'THE ULTIMATE GYM WORKOUT'

&

'YOUR POCKETBOOK GUIDE TO THE ULTIMATE GYM WORKOUT'

SO, IN A NUTSHELL:

QUESTION: WHAT WILL YOU GET OUT OF THIS BOOK?

ANSWER: A SHORT, STRAIGHT-TO-THE-POINT, NO BS FORMULA FOR ACHIEVING FAT LOSS AND MUSCLE GAIN WITHOUT RESORTING TO STEROIDS!

...AND HERE'S A HANDFUL OF TESTIMONIALS BEFORE WE START...

"The training and dieting regimes highlighted throughout this book are essential for success. Dr. Lee has extensive knowledge in this regard and clearly knows what he's talking about here."

CHRIS

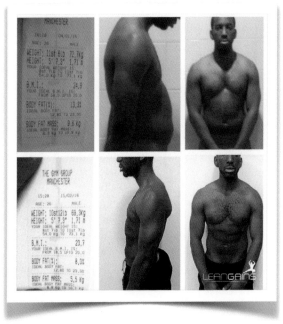

"I lost 8 pounds in 6 weeks and am more than happy with the results. Everything I did to get there is explained in thorough detail throughout this book!"

MICHAEL

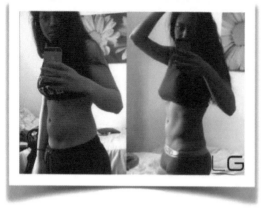

"I am so happy with these results! I've struggled in the past, but have finally reached may goals thanks to Dr. Lee's advice!"

SARA

"Being a personal trainer, Dr Lee's advice hits the nail on the head. **'How To Get The Perfect Body'** *is an effective, yet no-BS approach to burning fat and building muscle"*

JAMIE

*'**"How To Get The Perfect Body'** is an absolute must for those looking to make some 'lean gains!'"*

MOLLY

*'**"How To Get The Perfect Body'** contains everything you need to know in 100 pages. This book is an absolute must!!!'"*

JON

"I was over 21 stone, and I lost 12 stone in weight in under 2 years. The nutritional advice and dieting regimes in all of Dr. Lee's books are spot on! "

MICHELLE

*"As a female bodybuilder, I can say that **"The Ultimate Gym Workout"** is the perfect adjunct for those serious about gaining muscle and burning fat!"*

SIAN

...OKAY, SO LET'S GET STARTED SHALL WE....

CHAPTER 1

WHAT IS THE PERFECT BODY?

SO, WHAT EXACTLY IS THE 'PERFECT BODY?'

THERE ARE 2 WAYS BY WHICH THE 'PERFECT BODY' CAN BE DEFINED:

1) THE 'POLITICALLY-CORRECT', CROWD-PLEASING, NON-OFFENSIVE DEFINITION!!

OR

2) THE 'POLITICALLY-INCORRECT', SUPERFICIAL, POTENTIALLY OFFENSIVE DEFINITION!!

THE ('POLITICALLY-CORRECT') ANSWER:

"THE 'PERFECT' BODY IS THE ONE THAT ALLOWS ME, MYSELF, AND I TO ATTAIN PEACE OF MIND TODAY, TOMORROW, AND FOREVER MORE!!!"

THE 'POLITICALLY-INCORRECT' ANSWER:

THE FACT OF THE MATTER IS THAT MOST PEOPLE WANT TO LOOK ATHLETIC AND LEAN!!

THE PERFECT BODY IS QUITE SIMPLY THE ONE YOU'RE PREPARED TO SHOW OFF IF NEED BE. IT'S THE ONE THAT LOOKS BACK AT YOU IN THE MIRROR AND SAYS
(to quote Joey from "Friends") :

"SO, HOW YOU DOIN??"

...BUT WHAT DO Y'ALL THINK????...

...Let's do a little test shall we...

SO, FELLAS:

If you had to choose between the three 'body-types' below, which one would you pick?

(Let me guess, the guy in the <u>middle</u>??)

..AND LADIES:

If you had to choose between the two 'body-types' below, which one would you pick?

....Let me guess...
(the lady on the <u>right</u>??)

CHAPTER 2

HOW DO YOU GET THE PERFECT BODY?

LET'S LOOK AT WHERE YOU'RE AT!!

MOST PEOPLE ARE:

EITHER TOO FAT AND WANT TO BURN FAT,

OR

TOO THIN AND WANT TO BUILD MUSCLE,

OR

BOTH (ie. SKINNY FAT).

IN ORDER TO GET THE *'PERFECT BODY'* (ie. LOOK ATHLETIC AND LEAN), YOU NEED TO DO THE FOLLOWING:

1. BURN FAT

2. BUILD MUSCLE

3. REPEAT

…..IN OTHER WORDS…..

YOU NEED TO SCULPT THAT BODY BY BUILDING NEW MUSCLE WHILST CHISELLING AWAY THAT UNSIGHTLY FAT.

…SO IN THE UPCOMING CHAPTERS, WE'RE GONNA TALK ABOUT HOW TO BURN FAT AND BUILD NEW MUSCLE. WE WILL ALSO ANSWER THE MOST POPULAR QUESTION ON EARTH…..

..CAN WE DO BOTH AT THE SAME TIME????..

CHAPTER 3

HOW DO YOU BURN THAT UNSIGHTLY FAT?

SO, HOW DO YOU BURN FAT?

...NO MATTER WHAT
THEY TELL YOU..

YOU HAVE TO BURN _MORE_ CALORIES THAN YOU
CONSUME IN ORDER TO LOSE WEIGHT!!

...YOU SEE, ALL DIETS WORK WHEN YOU BURN
OFF MORE THAN YOU EAT!!....

IT'S ALL ABOUT

THE CALORIES!

DIET	WILL DIET WORK IF I EAT MORE CALORIES THAN I BURN?	WILL THIS DIET WORK IF I EAT FEWER CALORIES THAN I BURN?
ATKINS	NO	YES
PALEO	NO	YES
KETOGENIC	NO	YES
WEIGHT-WATCHERS	NO	YES
SLIMMING WORLD	NO	YES
5:2	NO	YES
16:8	NO	YES
ALKALINE	NO	YES
FLEXIBLE	NO	YES
ROSEMARY CONLEY	NO	YES
SLIM-FAST	NO	YES
SOUTH BEACH	NO	YES
VEGAN	NO	YES
WARRIOR DIET	NO	YES
CAMBRIDGE DIET	NO	YES

BUT WHAT IS

A CALORIE?

A 'calorie' is a unit of energy.

Calories in food provide energy in the form of heat so that our bodies can function.

WHEN WE EAT MORE CALORIES THAN WE BURN, THAT EXTRA ENERGY (OR CALORIES) IS STORED AS NEW FAT AND MUSCLE.

WHEN WE EAT FEWER CALORIES THAN WE BURN, THE BODY USES ITS ENERGY STORES (FAT AND MUSCLE) IN ORDER TO PROVIDE THE BODY WITH ENOUGH ENERGY TO STAY ALIVE.

THIS IS WHY MOST PEOPLE CANNOT BUILD NEW MUSCLE AND BURN FAT AT THE SAME TIME. THERE ARE SOME EXCEPTIONS (NEWBIES, STEROID USERS, OBESE PEOPLE).

SO WITH THAT IN MIND, WE SHOULD FOCUS ON THE CALORIES IF WE WANT TO REALLY BURN OFF THAT FAT!!

THIS DOES MEAN, HOWEVER, THAT WE NEED TO DO SOME MATHS BEFORE WE GET STARTED

..BY THE WAY, DON'T WORRY IF THIS BIT
SEEMS LONG-WINDED, IT'S WORTH IT!!!!!..

<u>FIRST</u>, LET'S SEE HOW MANY CALORIES
YOU EAT EACH AND EVERY DAY.

THESE CALORIES ARE CALLED
'MAINTENANCE CALORIES.'

THEY'RE GIVEN THIS NAME BECAUSE THEY'RE
THE NUMBER OF CALORIES YOU NEED TO
'<u>MAINTAIN</u>' YOUR CURRENT WEIGHT!!

CHAPTER 4

MAINTENANCE CALORIES

THERE ARE 2 WAYS TO CALCULATE MAINTENANCE CALORIES

METHOD A

THE LONG BUT MOST
ACCURATE METHOD

OR

METHOD B

THE QUICK BUT LEAST
ACCURATE METHOD

METHOD A

THE LONG BUT MOST ACCURATE WAY OF CALCULATING CALORIE MAINTENANCE

1. **<u>CALCULATE YOUR CURRENT WEIGHT</u>**

<u>TRACK YOUR WEIGHT FOR 14 DAYS</u>

WEIGH YOURSELF EVERYDAY
USING DIGITAL SCALES

DAY	WEEK 1 (Pounds)	WEEK 2 (Pounds)
MONDAY		
TUESDAY		
WEDNESDAY		
THURSDAY		
FRIDAY		
SATURDAY		
SUNDAY		

CALCULATE YOUR AVERAGE WEIGHT

ADD ALL OF THE 14 VALUES IN THE TABLE ON THE PREVIOUS PAGE, AND DIVIDE BY 14 TO WORK OUT YOUR AVERAGE WEIGHT

YOUR AVERAGE WEIGHT = _____ POUNDS

2. **CALCULATE YOUR MAINTENANCE CALORIES**

"THIS PART IS GOING TO BE SUPER-ANNOYING, BUT IS BY FAR THE MOST ACCURATE AND RELIABLE WAY OF ESTIMATING YOUR DAILY CALORIE REQUIREMENTS!"

YOU MUST:

*RECORD EVERYTHING YOU EAT EACH DAY USING 'MYFITNESSPAL' AND DIGITAL KITCHEN SCALES

....SO HERE'S WHAT YOU HAVE TO DO FOR THE NEXT TWO WEEKS!!....

CALCULATE YOUR AVERAGE DAILY CALORIES

DAY	WEEK 1 (Calories)	WEEK 2 (Calories)
MONDAY		
TUESDAY		
WEDNESDAY		
THURSDAY		
FRIDAY		
SATURDAY		
SUNDAY		

ADD ALL OF THE 14 VALUES IN THE TABLE ABOVE AND DIVIDE BY 14 TO WORK OUT YOUR AVERAGE DAILY CALORIES INTAKE.

YOUR AVERAGE DAILY CALORIES = _____ CALORIES

"WELL, THERE'S A MUCH QUICKER AND EASIER WAY TO ESTIMATE YOUR MAINTENANCE CALORIES....
AND YOU CAN DO IT IN LESS THAN 60 SECONDS!!!"

METHOD B

THE QUICK BUT LEAST ACCURATE WAY OF CALCULATING CALORIE MAINTENANCE

THE QUICK AND EASY WAY TO 'ESTIMATE' YOUR MAINTENANCE CALORIES

1. CALCULATE YOUR CURRENT WEIGHT

YOUR AVERAGE WEIGHT = _____ POUNDS

2. <u>ASSESS YOUR CURRENT ACTIVITY LEVELS</u>

HOW TO ASSESS ACTIVITY LEVELS

BODY WEIGHT MULTIPLIER	VALUE
SEDENTARY (NO ACTIVITY)	12
LIGHTLY ACTIVE	13.5
MODERATELY ACTIVE	15
VERY ACTIVE	16.5
EXTREMELY ACTIVE	17.5

LIGHTLY ACTIVE	MODERATELY ACTIVE
1-2 hours of weights and/or cardio exercise per week.	3-5 hours of weights and/or cardio exercise per week.
VERY ACTIVE	**EXTREMELY ACTIVE**
6-7 hours of weights and/or cardio exercise per week.	7+ hours of weights and/or cardio exercise per week.

CALCULATE YOUR
MAINTENANCE CALORIES

MAINTENANCE CALORIES (per day)

MAINTENANCE CALORIES (kcal)
= WEIGHT (lbs) x ACTIVITY VALUE

AN EXAMPLE OF HOW
THIS WOULD WORK

- BILL WEIGHS 200 POUNDS, GOES TO THE GYM AROUND 3 TIMES A WEEK AND JOGS AROUND THE BLOCK EVERY SO OFTEN.

- BILL HAS AN ACTIVITY LEVEL THEREFORE OF AROUND 15.

- BILL'S MAINTENANCE CALORIES ARE 200 X 15 = 3000kcal per day

CHAPTER 5

MACRONUTRIENT
RATIOS

KNOW YOUR MACROS

WHAT ARE MACRONUTRIENTS?

OVER 95% OF THE FOOD WE EAT CONSISTS OF
MACRONUTRIENTS (OR MACROS).

MACROS CONSIST OF:

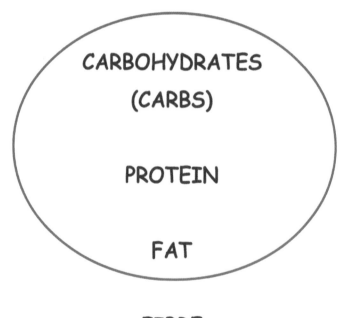

CARBOHYDRATES
(CARBS)

PROTEIN

FAT

FIBRE

(& ALCOHOL)

FOR SIMPLICITY, WE'RE ONLY GOING TO FOCUS ON CARBS, PROTEIN, FAT, AND TO SOME DEGREE, DIETARY FIBRE......!!

CARBOHYDRATES

FUNCTION	HEALTHY SOURCES
Carbs are an essential energy source. In other words, carbs will provide you with a ton of energy throughout the day and when you're training hard in the gym.	Pasta, Brown Rice, Sweet Potatoes, Fruits & Vegetables, Porridge, Couscous, Quinoa.

PROTEIN

FUNCTION	HEALTHY SOURCES
Protein has many important functions including making hormones, antibodies, hair, skin, and the list goes on. Our main concern, however, is muscle. If you don't eat enough protein, your muscle won't grow very much (if at all)!!	Beef, Red Meat, Chicken, Pork, Fish, Eggs, Soybeans, Nuts, Milk, Cheese, Yogurt, Lentils and Chia Seeds.

....IF WE GET OUR MACRONUTRIENT RATIO WRONG, WE WILL LOSE MUSCLE ESPECIALLY WHILST ON A CALORIE-DEFICIT!!!...

DIETARY FAT

FUNCTION	HEALTHY SOURCES
Fats have a vital role in energy storage. Nerve and brain function, cell and skin structure, transporting fat-soluble vitamins A, D, and E, steroid-hormone production, essential fatty acids, and muscle growth.	Fish, Avocado, Olive Oil, Cod Liver Oil and Nuts.

FIBRE

FUNCTION	HEALTHY SOURCES
Fibre is derived from plants and it does wonders for all the good bacteria that reside in your gut. Fibre also keeps you fuller for longer. This means that you don't need as many calories during the day (hence more fat-burning).	Fruits, Vegetables, Oats, Beans, Wholegrain, Nuts, Vegetables, Quinoa.

ATWATER FACTORS

- In order to workout how many calories need to come from the carbs, fats and proteins when bulking and cutting, you need to understand 'atwater' factors.

- Macronutrients have different calorie values.

- 1g of fat holds more calories [9kcal/g] than 1g of carbohydrate [4kcal] and 1g of protein [4kcal].

CALCULATE YOUR MACROS FOR MAINTAINING YOUR CURRENT WEIGHT

- As a general rule of thumb, we want to consume 0.3-0.5 grams per pound bodyweight of dietary fat (ideally from healthy sources already mentioned).

- We also want to aim for anything between 0.8 grams to 1gram per pound protein.

- On average, you want to be consuming around 30-40g fibre per day throughout the day in order to prevent hunger pangs. More specifically, for every 2000 calories, aim for 25-35g of fibre.

- The remaining calories will come from carbohydrates.

CALCULATE YOUR MACROS FOR MAINTAINING YOUR CURRENT WEIGHT

DIETARY FAT
(DAILY REQUIREMENTS)

= 0.3 x WEIGHT (lbs) = _____ grams/day

DIETARY FAT/DAY = GRAMS X 9

= _____ calories/day

DIETARY PROTEIN
(DAILY REQUIREMENTS)

= 1 x WEIGHT (lbs) = _____ grams/day

DIETARY PROTEIN/DAY = GRAMS X 4

= _____ calories/day

CALCULATE YOUR MACROS FOR MAINTAINING YOUR CURRENT WEIGHT

CARBOHYDRATES
(DAILY REQUIREMENTS)

TOTAL DAILY CALORIES - CALORIES FROM FAT & PROTEIN

= _____ calories/day

CARBOHYDRATES
(DAILY REQUIREMENTS)

CALORIES FROM CARBS ÷ 4

= _____ grams/day

YOUR NEW CALORIE AND MACRO REQUIREMENTS FOR MAINTENANCE

MACROS	WEIGHT (grams)	CALORIES (Kcal)
FAT		
PROTEIN		
CARBS		
TOTAL		

CHAPTER 6

IT'S NOW TIME TO BURN OFF THAT UNSIGHTLY FAT

IT'S TIME TO BURN FAT!!

To successfully and predictably burn fat and keep it off in the long term, you have to <u>cut your calorie intake</u>. You don't want to cut calories too much otherwise you'll

<u>crash-and-burn</u>.

A safe reduction is around

15% below maintenance.

We also want to get the right amount of carbs, protein, and fat into our diet. If we get the ratio of these macronutrients wrong, we will lose fat, but we'll also lose a lot of muscle!!

CALORIE-TO-GRAM CONVERTOR

Remember the 'Atwater Factors.' I've summarised them in the table below:

GRAMS	CALORIES
1g CARBOHYDRATE	4
1g PROTEIN	4
1g FAT	9

1. <u>CALCULATE CALORIE REQUIREMENTS FOR FAT LOSS</u>

CALORIES TO BURN FAT

=

0.85 X MAINTENANCE CALORIES

THIS WILL ENABLE YOU TO LOSE ROUGHLY <u>1-2 POUNDS</u> BODY FAT PER WEEK!!

CALORIES TO BURN FAT
= _____ CALORIES

2. CALCULATE YOUR FAT/PROTEIN REQUIREMENTS FOR FAT LOSS

DIETARY FAT
(DAILY REQUIREMENTS)

= 0.3 x WEIGHT (lbs) = _____ grams/day

DIETARY FAT/DAY = GRAMS X 9

= _____ calories/day

DIETARY PROTEIN
(DAILY REQUIREMENTS)

= 1 x WEIGHT (lbs) = _____ grams/day

DIETARY PROTEIN/DAY = GRAMS X 4

= _____ calories/day

3. <u>CALCULATE YOUR MACROS</u>
<u>FOR FAT LOSS</u>

<u>CARBOHYDRATES</u>
<u>(DAILY REQUIREMENTS)</u>

**TOTAL DAILY CALORIES - CALORIES
FROM FAT & PROTEIN**

= _____ calories/day

<u>CARBOHYDRATES</u>
<u>(DAILY REQUIREMENTS)</u>

CALORIES FROM CARBS ÷ 4

= _____ grams/day

4. <u>NEW CALORIE AND MACRO REQUIREMENTS FOR FAT LOSS</u>

MACROS	WEIGHT (grams)	CALORIES (Kcal)
FAT		
PROTEIN		
CARBS		
TOTAL		

LET'S LOOK AT AN EXAMPLE HERE

AMY FEELS OVERWEIGHT AND WANTS TO LOSE FAT <u>WITHOUT</u> LOSING MUSCLE!!

Amy feels Overweight and Desperately Wants to Burn Fat WITHOUT Losing Muscle!

So, let's take a look at Amy. She wants to burn fat! Amy weighs 200 pounds and consumes 2500 calories per day.

<u>STEP 1</u>:

AMY'S CURRENT CALORIE INTAKE AND WEIGHT

WEIGHT: 200 pounds

DAILY CALORIES: 2500 calories

STEP 2:

AMY'S CALORIC REQUIREMENT

FOR BURNING FAT

(in Calories)

15% reduction from 2500

2500 x 0.85 = 2125

Therefore, Amy needs 2125 calories per day in order to successfully lose weight.

STEP 3:

CALCULATE AMY'S MACRONUTRIENT REQUIREMENTS FOR BURNING FAT:

PROTEIN (grams)

Protein Requirements = 1g/pound

Amy's Protein Requirements = 200g

FAT (grams)

Fat Requirements = 0.3g/pound

Amy's Fat Requirements = 60g

STEP 4:

CALORIE-TO-GRAM CONVERTOR:

PROTEIN REQUIREMENTS = 200g X 4 = <u>**800 Calories**</u>

FAT REQUIREMENTS = 60g X 9 = <u>**540 Calories**</u>

AMY'S MACRO REQUIREMENTS	GRAMS	CALORIES
PROTEIN	200g Protein	800
FAT	60g Fat	540

STEP 5:

NEW CARBOHYDRATE REQUIREMENT (calories)

1. TOTAL CALORIES FOR

FAT LOSS = <u>2125 calories</u>

2. CALORIES FOR PROTEIN & FAT

= 540+800 = <u>1340 calories</u>

3. CALORIES FOR CARBS = 2125-1340

CALORIES FOR CARBS = <u>785 calories</u>

<u>STEP 6</u>:

NEW CARBOHYDRATE REQUIREMENT (grams)

CALORIES FOR CARBS = 785 calories

CARBS REQUIREMENTS IN GRAMS = 785/4

CARB REQUIREMENTS IN GRAMS = <u>196g</u>

SUMMARY

So, in conclusion, in order to burn fat and minimise muscle loss, Amy needs:

CALORIES	PROTEIN	FAT	CARBS
2125	200g (800cal)	60g (540cal)	196g (785cal)

> REPEAT THIS EVERY 2-3 MONTHS OR SO IN ORDER TO AVOID ADAPTION.

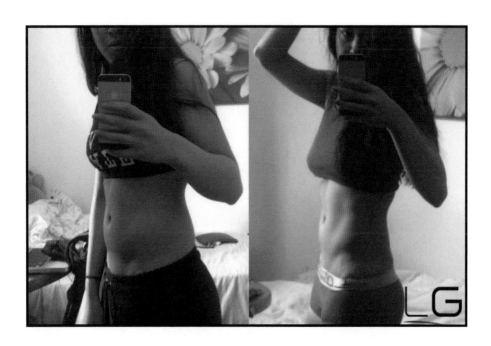

· NOW THAT AMY KNOWS EXACTLY HOW MANY CALORIES AND HOW MUCH PROTEIN, FAT, AND CARBS SHE NEEDS, SHE CAN USE THESE FIGURES TO HELP DESIGN A SERIES OF MEAL PLANS (SEE CHAPTER 9).

· ONCE SHE'S DONE THIS, ALL SHE HAS TO DO IS STICK TO THE MEAL PLANS.

CHAPTER 7

HOW TO BUILD NEW MUSCLE WITH MINIMAL FAT

WHAT'S NEEDED TO BUILD AND MAINTAIN <u>NEW</u> MUSCLE?

- CALORIE-SURPLUS
- MACRONUTRIENTS
- MICRONUTRIENTS
- TESTOSTERONE
- EXERCISE
- SLEEP/REST

1. <u>NUTRITIONAL REQUIREMENTS</u> FOR MUSCLE GROWTH

- To successfully and predictably maximise muscle growth, you do have to eat more than you burn (in other words, you have to be on a calorie-surplus).

- Although there are instances whereby you <u>**can**</u> gain muscle whilst burning fat (such as when you're **new** to weight-training for instance), you ideally want to be on a calorie-surplus if long-term muscle growth is a priority.

- However, in order to **minimise <u>fat gain</u>**, try to limit calorie intake to 10% above maintenance.

CALORIE-TO-GRAM CONVERTOR

Remember the 'Atwater Factors.'

I've summarised them in the table below:

GRAMS	CALORIES
1g CARBOHYDRATE	4
1g PROTEIN	4
1g FAT	9

1. <u>CALCULATE CALORIE</u> <u>REQUIREMENTS FOR FAT LOSS</u>

CALORIES TO BUILD <u>NEW</u> MUSCLE
=
1.1 X MAINTENANCE CALORIES

THIS WILL ENABLE YOU TO BUILD NEW MUSCLE WHILST MINIMISING ADDITIONAL FAT GAIN!!!

CALORIES TO GROW MUSCLE

= _____ CALORIES

2. CALCULATE YOUR FAT/PROTEIN REQUIREMENTS FOR FAT LOSS

DIETARY FAT
(DAILY REQUIREMENTS)

= 0.3 x WEIGHT (lbs)
=
_____ grams/day

DIETARY FAT/DAY = GRAMS X 9

= _____ calories/day

DIETARY PROTEIN
(DAILY REQUIREMENTS)

= 1 x WEIGHT (lbs)
=
_____ grams/day

DIETARY FAT/DAY = GRAMS X 4

= _____ calories/day

3. <u>CALCULATE YOUR CARBOHYDRATE REQUIREMENTS FOR FAT LOSS</u>

<u>CARBOHYDRATE</u>
<u>DAILY REQUIREMENTS</u>

TOTAL DAILY CALORIES
- (CALORIES FROM FAT & PROTEIN)

= _____ calories/day

<u>CARBOHYDRATE</u>
<u>(DAILY REQUIREMENTS)</u>

CALORIES FROM CARBS ÷ 4

= _____ carbs g/day

4. NEW CALORIE AND MACRO REQUIREMENTS FOR MUSCLE GROWTH

MACROS	WEIGHT (grams)	CALORIES (Kcal)
FAT		
PROTEIN		
CARBS		
TOTAL		

LET'S LOOK AT AN EXAMPLE HERE

KEVIN FEELS THIN & WEAK. HE DESPERATELY WANTS TO BUILD MUSCLE WHILST GAINING MINIMAL FAT!!

Kevin weighs 200 pounds and consumes 2500 calories per day.

STEP 1:

KEVIN'S CURRENT CALORIE INTAKE AND WEIGHT

WEIGHT: 200 pounds

DAILY CALORIES: 2500 calories

STEP 2:

KEVIN'S CALORIC REQUIREMENT FOR BURNING FAT (in Calories)

10% increase from 2500

2500 x 1.1 = 2750

Therefore, Kevin needs 2750 calories per day in order to successfully lose weight.

STEP 3:

CALCULATE KEVIN'S MACRONUTRIENT REQUIREMENTS FOR BUILDING MUSCLE:

PROTEIN (grams)

Protein Requirements = 1g/pound

Kevin's Protein Needs = 200g

FAT (grams)

Fat Requirements = 0.3g/pound

Kevin's Fat Requirements = 60g

STEP 4:

CALORIE-TO-GRAM CONVERTOR:

PROTEIN REQUIREMENTS

= 200g X 4 = 800 Calories

FAT REQUIREMENTS

= 60g X 9 = 540 Calories

KEVIN'S MACRO REQUIREMENTS	GRAMS	CALORIES
PROTEIN	200g Protein	800
FAT	60g Fat	540

STEP 5:

NEW CARBOHYDRATE REQUIREMENT

(calories)

TOTAL CALORIES FOR MUSCLE GROWTH

= 2750 calories

CALORIES FOR PROTEIN & FAT = 540+800

= 1340

CALORIES FOR CARBS = 2750-1340

CALORIES FOR CARBS = 1410

STEP 6:

NEW CARBOHYDRATE REQUIREMENT (grams)

CALORIES FOR CARBS = 1410 calories

CARBS REQUIREMENTS IN GRAMS = 1410/4

CARB REQUIREMENTS IN GRAMS = 352

SUMMARY

So, in conclusion, in order to build muscle

with minimal fat, Kevin needs:

CALORIES	PROTEIN	FAT	CARBS
2750	200g (800cal)	60g (540cal)	352g (1410cal)

2. <u>WHAT ABOUT MICRONUTRIENTS?</u>

Micronutrients consist of vitamins and minerals.

In other words, they are the vitamins and minerals that are needed in small amounts to help the processing of the macronutrients into a healthy and active body.

Consuming your daily requirements are essential for optimal health and well-being.

You're going to have a hard time growing and maintaining new muscle if you don't consume enough micronutrients. It is beyond the realm of this book to go into the specific role of each and every micronutrient out there.

In a nutshell, however, please
remember the following:

1. Vitamins B, C, D, and E are essential for active people who train regularly.

2. B-Vitamins provide energy.

3. Vitamins C and E help to prevent muscle loss, especially in times of stress.

4. Vitamin D is essential for muscle growth and testosterone production.

5. Calcium, zinc, iron, and phosphorous, are essential for muscle-growth.

6. Sodium, magnesium, and potassium are essential for endurance, recovery, and overall performance.

3. TESTOSTERONE

Testosterone is VITAL for muscle growth and fat-burning, and optimal sexual health in men (and women).

Testosterone levels drop approx 1% each year over the age of 30.

You can BOOST your testosterone levels by doing the following:

- **Sleep 7-8 hours per night.**
- **Resistance/Weight Training.**
- **Eat Enough Protein (1g/pound).**
- **Eat Enough Fat (0.3-0.5g/pound)**
- **Eat Enough Micronutrients.**
- **Eat Enough Carbs If You're Training.**

4. <u>EXERCISE</u>

"We do not stop exercising because we grow old. We grow old because we stop exercising."

Kenneth Cooper

If you're not already doing so, then you really must adopt an exercise routine and stick to it.

Now, although most exercises out there will allow us to live longer, weight training is the best way to grow NEW muscle and minimise fat gain.

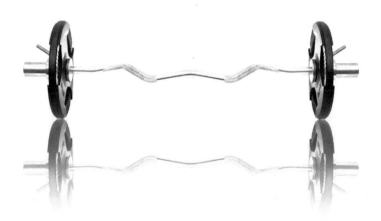

TOP 10 BENEFITS OF WEIGHT TRAINING

1. Increases Muscle Strength

Increases muscle strength which makes it easier to not only lift heavier weights, but also become, look and feel stronger outside the gym too.

2. Increases Metabolic Rate

Increases your muscle-to-fat ratio. One pound of fat burns approximately 2 calories a day whereas 1 pound of muscle burns approximately 6 calories per day. Therefore, the more muscle you have, the more energy you burn at rest and hence a higher metabolic rate.

3. Stronger Joints and Bones

Makes your joints and bones stronger, and also reduces risk of osteoporosis. Peak bone mass is achieved in adulthood and then begins a slow decline. Weight training maintains healthy bone mass as you get older.

4. Improves Body Awareness, Balance and Coordination

When you weight train, you will over time develop a better mind-to-muscle connection. This improves your coordination and balance outside of the gym.

5. Allows for Physical Change and Control of Body Shape

Weight training is the only form of exercise that can allow you to physically change your body shape. If you want a bigger chest or bigger arm muscles, for instance, weight training can make that possible.

6. Improves Mood

More of the 'happy, feel-good' hormones are released after weight training including serotonin, endorphins and dopamine.

7. Boosts Confidence

Your confidence goes through the roof once you get into a well-designed weight training programme.

8. Improves Physical Appearance
and Makes You Look Younger

Not only contributes towards fat loss, but also

improves skin tone. Most trainees who lift weights and exercise on the whole tend to have younger looking skin which appears more elastic, smooth and supple. The improved muscle tone also reduces the risk of saggy skin.

9. Improves Muscle Preservation As You Age

After the age of 30, most people start to lose approximately 3 to 5% of their muscle per decade. This is known as sarcopenia and comes with a whole host of potential health problems as you age including diabetes, weight gain, dementia, depression, etc. The good news is that weight training can prevent and even reverse sarcopenia.

10. Improves Brain Function and Memory

Increases blood flow to the brain as well as improving cognitive ability. This means that weight lifting can help you remember and focus on things much better.

HOW TO PLAN YOUR WEIGHT TRAINING SESSIONS

- There are '**BIG**' muscles (such as chest, back, and legs) and there are '**SMALL**' muscles (such as triceps, abs, calves).

- **As a general rule of thumb,** you want to do approximately:

  ✳ 60-120 reps per week for the bigger muscle groups.
  ✳ 30-60 reps per week for the smaller muscles.

- These guidelines provide you with a certain degree of flexibility regarding how you set up your training week.

- For instance, for each session in the gym, if you're training your chest (for example), you can train:
  - ✳ Once a week in the 60-120 rep range,
  - ✳ Twice a week in the 30-60 rep range, or
  - ✳ Three times a week in the 15-30 rep range.

- Training the **'big' muscles** twice a week and the **'small' muscles** two to four times a week is generally advised.

HOW DOES LIFTING WEIGHTS GROW MUSCLE?

- **Weight-training** creates trauma and physical stress within the muscle. Whilst you're recovering and resting after a workout, the muscle grows bigger as part of a compensatory mechanism to withstand similar stresses in the future.

1. Progressive Tension Overload

Progressive Tension Overload is defined as lifting or pushing more weight or doing more reps than you did previously. For instance, if last month, you could only bench press 50kg but now you can bench press 60kg; or doing 10 reps of the same weight one week and 12 the following week.

The human body is very adaptive, and in order for muscle growth to continue, the muscles need to be continuously challenged. **Progressive overload is the best and most effective** means of physically stimulating muscle growth.

2. <u>Time-Under-Tension and Cellular Fatigue</u>

You can either lift weights really quickly or really slowly. You'll struggle to do a lot of reps if you're lifting/pushing weights slowly as opposed to quickly. The movement starts off easy, but after a while becomes unbearable. This is known as 'cellular fatigue.'

'Time-under-tension' is the length of time that muscle is under stress. In other words, the longer it takes you to perform a single rep, the greater the amount of 'time-under-tension.'

To understand the relevance of this, we have to take a quick look at **concentric and eccentric contractions.**

A **concentric contraction** causes muscles to shorten, thereby generating force. **Eccentric contractions** cause muscles to elongate.

An example of an eccentric contraction is the downward movement during a barbell curl.

Whilst the muscle is in its eccentric phase, it is being stretched and damaged. It is theorised that the longer the eccentric phase, the more muscle damage that occurs. More muscle is therefore laid down during rest/recovery. The obvious problem, however, is that it becomes harder to apply progressive tension over load, in the long term, when you're making each rep twice as long.

3. <u>So, What's The Conclusion?</u>

Both principles (progressive overload and time-under-tension) can be applied during your weight-training workouts!!!

"I would apply progressive overload to your low-rep 'heavy-lifting' weight sessions and apply time-under-tension to your 'light-weight-lifting' sessions."

Dr Jonathan S Lee

LIFTING HEAVY vs LIFTING LIGHT

- 'Lifting Heavy Weights' means doing a low number of reps with a heavy weight and longer rest periods (eg. 4-6 reps and 3 minute rest period between sets).

- 'Lifting Light Weights' means doing a relatively high number of reps with a lighter weight and shorter rest periods (eg. 10-15 reps with 1-2 minute rest periods).

- Despite what you may have heard, when it comes to muscle growth, you can grow and maintain muscle lifting light weights as well as heavy weights. They are both effective for muscle growth.

- Ultimately, muscle growth occurs during rest/ sleep after you've sufficiently stimulated the muscle by subjecting it to a 'heavy' load (ie. weight training).

- Many trainees accept that this means lifting/ pushing heavy weights will stimulate muscle growth. Light weights, at one point, were thought not to sufficiently stimulate muscle growth. However, lifting to near failure using light weights has been shown to stimulate a significant amount of muscle growth!

- The main advantages of lifting heavy weights on a regular basis are that it allows for relatively shorter workouts (despite longer rest periods) since you hit your threshold much quicker. It also makes your muscles much stronger as well as physically bigger.

- The main advantages of lifting light weights on a regular basis are that they allow beginners to optimise their form and develop a muscle-mind connection. This cannot and should not be attempted using heavy weights if you're new to a training programme.

- Lifting light weights also allows for a safer and better control of the weight if you decide to return the weight SLOWLY back to starting position (something known as '**time under tension**').

- Lifting lighter weights is often strongly recommended for small muscles such as the 'rotatory cuff' muscles.

- This really is just the tip of the iceberg though. There's a lot more to it than that. I go over this topic in immense detail in my other books **'Lean Gains' (2nd Edition)** and **'The Essential Guide to Sports Nutrition and Bodybuilding.'**

- However, the <u>take home message</u> here is that **both heavy and light weights have their place.** As a rule of thumb, once you've warmed up, start your sessions with heavy weights and finish off with light weights.

"THE ULTIMATE GYM WORKOUT"

(and the pocketbook version) sets in place a series of tried-and-tested workout regimes specifically designed to provide the gym-enthusiast with tailored workouts suited for BOTH men and women.

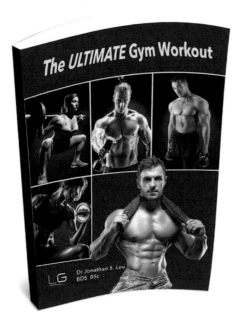
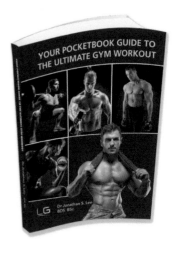

AVAILABLE FROM:

(www.leangains.co.uk)

or

Amazon

CHAPTER 8

CARDIOVASCULAR EXERCISE

WHAT ABOUT CARDIO?

Cardiovascular exercise (cardio) is any activity that increases heart rate and respiration while using large muscle groups repetitively and rhythmically.

We Can Do:

1. High-Intensity-Interval Training

2. Low-Intensity (Steady-State) Cardio.

1. High-Intensity-Interval Training (HIIT)

- **HIIT** involves work periods ranging from 30 seconds to three minutes. A classic HIIT workout would require working between 80-100% of your maximum heart rate with short rest intervals in-between.

2. Low-Intensity (Steady-State) Cardio

- Almost any form of exercise that you can sustain for over 30 minutes can be classed as **steady-state cardio,** and can do wonders for your fitness.

- Examples include walking, jogging on a treadmill, rowing machines, cycling machines, etc.

The PROS of HIIT

❖ Burns same number of calories as low-intensity cardio in less time.

❖ Improves aerobic and anaerobic endurance. This improves performance in other sports eg. Football, basketball, sprinting, etc.

❖ Increases blood-flow to muscles, helps burn and break down stubborn fat, makes joints and tendons more supple.

❖ Burns loads of calories (One single HIIT session can burn upwards of 300 calories!!!).

❖ Creates an environment whereby you're burning extra calories for a few days after [This is known as excess post-exercise oxygen consumption (or EPOC)].

The CONS of HIIT

❖   More chance of injury from acute stress and pressure on joints and tendons.

❖   Not suitable for those with heart problems.

❖   Not always suitable for beginners. Because of the intense nature of HIIT, trainees should ideally have some previous experience and wean their way onto HIIT.

❖ HIIT will compromise muscle growth when done too often. 1-2 HIIT sessions per week should suffice, especially if you're weight-training over 4 days a week.

❖ It's an additional tool for accentuating fat-loss whilst dieting, but is no match when compared to adopting weight training and a healthy calorie-deficit to your routine.

The PROS of STEADY-STATE CARDIO

❖ Suitable for beginners, and people who are new to the gym/exercise or people with injuries or joint problems.

❖ Suitable for those with a history of heart disease or cardiovascular disease.

❖ Steady-state cardio is an excellent way of burning calories without overtaxing the body.

The CONS of STEADY-STATE CARDIO

❖ Longer duration of exercise is required to achieve significant fat loss.

❖ Performing low-intensity cardio too often can be catabolic and adversely interferes with muscle growth.

❖ It can be extremely boring spending 45 minutes on a treadmill. Other more enjoyable forms of steady-state cardio may include a brisk walk or jog outside.

BABY STEPS ARE EVERYTHING!!

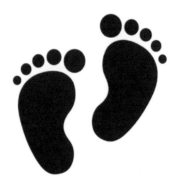

❖ If you're new to cardio, as with diet and weight training, it's best to introduce the routines gradually so as to not overwhelm your body. Doing so can potentially lead to a drop in metabolic rate in addition to muscle loss.

❖ In other words, you should aim to progress gradually. For example, if in your first week, you decide to walk for 10 minutes twice a week, progress to 15 minutes the following week; and maybe a 10 minute jog the week after. A **gradual** progression in intensity is key for long term success.

5. SLEEP/REST

What's The Big Deal About Sleep?

The brain is directly and indirectly responsible for literally everything we do even when we're sleeping. So, whatever it is we decide to do once we're awake, we do **worse** when we're sleep-deprived.

With regards to muscle gain and fat loss, prolonged sleep deprivation can literally destroy your progress

IN EVERY SENSE OF THE WORD!!

Sleeping For 5 Hours or Less:

❖   Testosterone levels drop.

❖   Cortisol levels rise.

❖   Growth Hormone levels drop.

❖   Less Leptin Produced.

❖   More Ghrelin Release.

.....So, what does all that mean???....

SO, WHAT HAPPENS WHEN YOU'RE SLEEP-DEPRIVED??

- ❖ More Abdominal Fat Gain

- ❖ Increased Muscle Loss

- ❖ Energy Levels Drop

- ❖ More Hunger Pangs

- ❖ Less Concentration and Focus

- ❖ Less Motivation to Perform Exercise.

In fact, **The University of Chicago** did an experiment whereby 2 groups of subjects were both put on a calorie-restricted diet for 2 weeks.

The only difference was that one group slept for 5 hours and the other group slept for 8 hours. At the end of the study, the group with only 5 hours sleep lost 55% less body fat and 60% more muscle mass than the group that got 8 hours sleep.

• **So you really want to aim for 7-8 hours.**

CHAPTER 9

MEAL
PLANNING

THE METHOD BEHIND
THE MADNESS!!!

- The very definition of 'hell on earth' (as far as I'm concerned) revolves around the idea of whipping out your phone/notepad and recording the number of calories, or the amount of protein, fibre, carbs, and fat you're about to consume whenever it comes to meal time (or even snack time).

THIS IS WHERE MEAL PLANNING COMES IN!!

- The convenient alternative to counting calories every day for the rest of your life is to incorporate them into a series of meals throughout the day.

...SO NO MORE CALORIE COUNTING THEN?? ...THAT'S GREAT!!...

- In a nutshell, once you've calculated how many daily calories and macronutrients you need to burn fat, gain muscle, or even maintain your current weight (depending on what your goals are), you can **apply** these values to the meals you eat each day that add up to that number.

- For instance, if you require 1500 calories per day to lose weight, then you can design a meal plan that would add up to 1500 calories. The same would be true with the macronutrients. For example, if you need 200g protein per day, you can design meals that contain enough protein to provide you with 200g protein per day.

If you're looking to implement your daily calorie/
macro requirements into a series of meal plans,
then my <u>new</u> recipe book '<u>Lean Meals for Everyone</u>'
is definitely for you.

✦ Over 200 diverse, tasty, and above all
healthy recipes to choose from.

✦ Categorised calorie-based recipes and meal
plans taking away the need to count
calories.

✦ A wide range of recipes provides something
for everyone.

✦ An introduction to specific dieting regimes
at the start of each section.

✦ Foods and fluids you can consume to reduce
bloating and excess water retention.

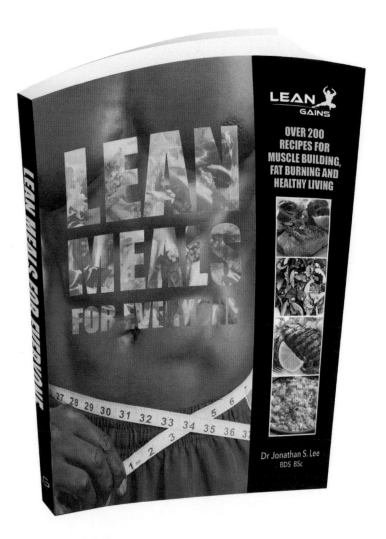

"LEAN MEALS FOR EVERYONE"

AVAILABLE FROM:

(www.leangains.co.uk)

or

Amazon

CHAPTER 10

PUTTING ALL THE
PIECES TOGETHER

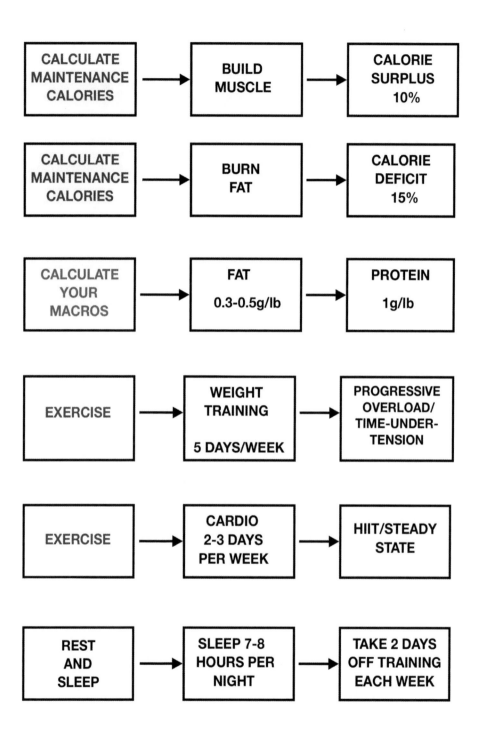

SO, THERE
YOU HAVE IT!!!

BURN FAT - CUT CALORIES!

BUILD MUSCLE - EAT MORE & LIFT WEIGHTS

REPEAT CYCLES OF BULKING AND CUTTING

DO THIS LONG ENOUGH,
AND YOU WILL GET
'THE PERFECT BODY!'

IT'S NOT ROCKET SCIENCE NOW IS IT?
EVEN LITTLE CHRIS GETS IT

....SO DID THIS BOOK COVER EVERYTHING YOU NEED TO KNOW??...

Well, everything I have discussed throughout this book is based on a plethora of scientific studies. In addition to decades of anecdotal research, as well as personal experience, I can guarantee success in this regard.

In other words,

if and when you apply the advice highlighted throughout this book, you **will** get the results you've been looking for!!

However, you will also inevitably face some obstacles along the way. There are certainly other factors we need to consider here.

..THERE ARE OTHER THINGS YOU NEED TO CONSIDER...

- SUPPLEMENTS
- WEIGHT-LOSS PLATEAUS
- REST PERIODS
- TRAINING FREQUENCY
- DIET BREAKS
- REFEEDS
- GUT BACTERIA
- WATER
- TRAINING INTENSITY

- MOTIVATION
- CONSISTENCY
- PLANT-BASED FOODS
- EATING MEAT
- FASTING
- HORMONES
- BLOATING
- MUSCLE GROWTH
- AGE
- BRAIN ACTIVITY

..........AND SOME OTHER STUFF.........

..THIS IS WHY I CAME UP WITH THE 'LEAN GAINS BOOK COLLECTION'...

As you can no-doubt imagine, it's **impossible** to squeeze **absolutely everything** into one book. This is why, over the last 8 years, I've been able to successfully spread this information throughout **6 books** in total.

I refer to these books as

'The Lean Gains Book Collection.'

If you would like to learn more about burning fat and building muscle, as well as how to overcome the obstacles mentioned on page 121, then I would suggest checking out **'Lean Gains (2nd Edition)'** and/or **'The Essential Guide to Sports Nutrition and Bodybuilding.'** These books cover the aforementioned topics in more detail.

— CHAPTER 11 —

THE
'LEAN GAINS'
BOOK COLLECTION

THE ESSENTIAL GUIDE TO SPORTS NUTRITION AND BODYBUILDING

'The Essential Guide to Sports Nutrition and Bodybuilding' contains **everything** you need to know about losing weight, eating right, gaining muscle, feeling great, and living a long, healthy, and vibrant life.

Outstanding Features include:

- **800 pages** of attractive, easy-to-digest information covering a huge range of topics.

- **Science-backed information** and advice based on over **580 clinical studies and references**.

- Over **254 full-colour photographs** and illustrations.

- Simple descriptions, paragraph breaks, and a **key-point summary** at the end of each chapter to allow for enjoyable reading.

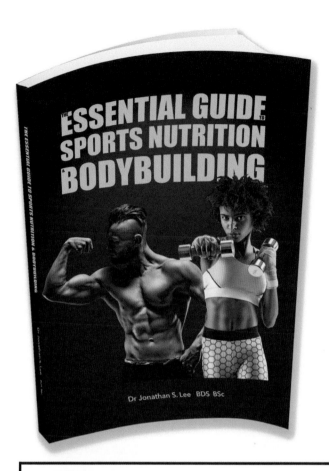

HARDBACK:	£64.99
PAPERBACK:	£49.99
E-BOOK:	£9.99

(prices may vary)

AVAILABLE AT

WWW.LEANGAINS.CO.UK

and

Amazon

LEAN GAINS
(2nd Edition)

'Lean Gains (2nd edition)' is an absolute MUST for those who are struggling to burn fat, bulk up, and break through weight-loss plateaus. I have created a comprehensive blueprint to help manage your weight and achieve faster results than you would using conventional dieting methods.

Outstanding Features include:

- **470 pages** of **easy-to-digest** information relating to the science behind fat-loss and muscle gain.

- **Science-backed information** and advice based on over **500 clinical studies and references**.

- Over **200 full-colour photographs** and illustrations.

- **Paragraph breaks**, colour pictures on almost every page, and a gentle sense of humour for enjoyable reading.

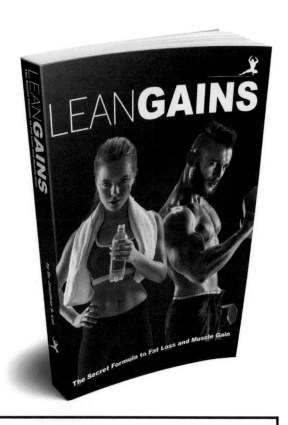

HARDBACK:	£49.99
PAPERBACK:	£45.99
EBOOK:	£9.99
AUDIOBOOK	£9.99

(prices may vary)

AVAILABLE AT

WWW.LEANGAINS.CO.UK

and

Amazon

THE ULTIMATE GYM WORKOUT

'**The Ultimate Gym Workout**' is the perfect adjunct to your gym workouts. This book sets in place a series of effective, tried-and-tested gym workouts. Designated set ranges, rep ranges, rest periods, and stretching routines take away the need to focus on anything other than the workouts themselves.

Outstanding Features include:

- **155 full-colour photographs and illustrations.**

- Detailed **weight-training** and **cardio workouts**.

- Simple descriptions and video links (ebook version).

- **Exercise routines** tailored for both **men and women**.

- **Stretching routines** tailored for both **men and women**.

- Choice between **3-day and 5-day workouts**.

- All exercises are **fully explained** and **illustrated**.

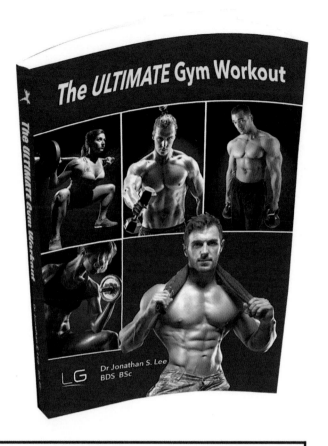

HARDBACK:	N/A
PAPERBACK:	£44.99
EBOOK:	£9.99

(prices may vary)

AVAILABLE AT

WWW.LEANGAINS.CO.UK

and

Amazon

YOUR POCKETBOOK GUIDE TO THE ULTIMATE GYM WORKOUT

'Your Pocketbook Guide to The Ultimate Gym Workout' is the 'pocketbook' accompaniment to its larger parent book
'The Ultimate Gym Workout.'

This book sets in place a series of effective tried-and-tested gym workouts.

Outstanding Features include:

- Detailed **weight-training** and **cardio workouts**.

- Simple descriptions and video links (ebook version).

- **Exercise routines** tailored for both **men and women**.

- Choice between **3-day and 5-day workouts**.

- All exercises are **fully explained** and **illustrated**.

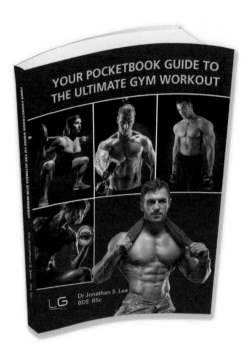

HARDBACK:	**N/A**
PAPERBACK:	**£14.99**
EBOOK:	**£9.99**

(prices may vary)

AVAILABLE AT

WWW.LEANGAINS.CO.UK

and

Amazon

HOW TO GET THE PERFECT BODY

'How to Get The Perfect Body' is a no-BS introduction to the world of diet and fitness.

'How To Get The Perfect Body' is extremely easy on the eye, contains a plethora of paragraph breaks, images, before & after pictures, and **can be read from front to back in less than an hour.**

However, this book contains **calculations and formulae** used by most fitness models and bodybuilders that you **will not** find in most fitness books.

By the time you've finished reading this book, you will know exactly how to achieve that **sexy** body you've been craving for all this time

No exercise routines are contained within this book.

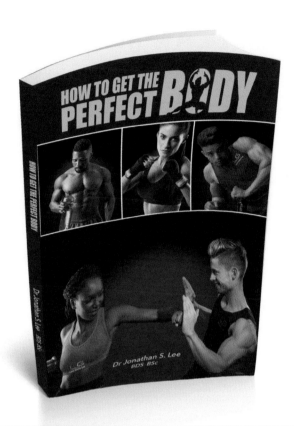

HARDBACK:	N/A
PAPERBACK:	£14.99
EBOOK:	£9.99

(prices may vary)

AVAILABLE AT

WWW.LEANGAINS.CO.UK

and

Amazon

LEAN MEALS
FOR EVERYONE

Eating regimes and dieting habits vary massively from one person to the next. Some dieters, for instance, prefer a ketogenic approach, whilst others may prefer to go vegan.

Some trainees prefer a calorie-based eating regime, whilst others feel more comfortable fasting for prolonged periods of time. The point is that one set of fixed meal plans is very unlikely to cater for everyone.

I wrote **'Lean Meals for Everyone'** as a means of addressing these issues.

This book contains a **wide range** of healthy and nutritious recipes and meal plans that will suit specific caloric and nutritional requirements regardless of diet.

HARDBACK:	N/A
PAPERBACK:	£29.99
EBOOK:	£9.99

(prices may vary)

AVAILABLE AT

WWW.LEANGAINS.CO.UK

and

Amazon

AND THAT'S ALL FOLKS!!

"Thank you so much for taking time out to read this book. I sincerely hope you find the principles covered throughout to be useful, and I wish you the very best moving forwards."

DR JONATHAN S. LEE

YOUR FEEDBACK IS IMPORTANT TO US!

If you like what you've read, then please take a minute to write a few words on Amazon about this book. I check all my reviews and love to receive feedback.

If you have any queries, questions, or concerns about anything, on the other hand, then please feel free to drop me an email at jon@leangains.co.uk and we will try our best to resolve your issue.

REFERENCES

PAPERS

1. McDonald L. "The Ultimate Diet 2.0."

2. Juleen R Zierath and John A Hawley. "Skeletal Muscle Fiber Type: Influence on Contractile and Metabolic Properties" *PLoS Biol. 2004 Oct; 2(10)*. Available at:https://www.ncbi.nlm.nih.gov/pmc/articles/PMC521732/

3. Ptdirect. "Skeletal Muscle – Anatomy and Fibre Types." Available at: https://www.ptdirect.com/training-design/anatomy-and-physiology/skeletal-muscle-2013-anatomy-and-fiber-types

4. Plowman SA et al. "Exercise physiology for health, fitness and performance." Boston, Mass; *Allyn and Bacon, 1997:433*

5. Kraemer WJ, Fleck SJ, Evans WJ. "Strength and power training: physiological mechanisms of adaptation." *Exercise and Sport Sciences Reviews [01 Jan 1996, 24:363-397]*. Available at: http://europepmc.org/abstract/med/8744256

6. G. R. Adams, B. M. Hather, K. M. Baldwin, and G. A. Dudley. "Skeletal muscle myosin heavy chain composition and resistance training." *J Applied Physiology*. Available at: https://www.physiology.org/doi/abs/10.1152/jappl.1993.74.2.911

7. Thorstensson A, Sjödin B, Karlsson J. "Enzyme activities and muscle strength after "sprint training" in man." *Food Science and Technology International*. Available at:https://www.ncbi.nlm.nih.gov/pubmed/170792

8. R H Edwards D K Hill D A Jones P A Merton. "Fatigue of long duration in human skeletal muscle after exercise." Available at: https://physoc.onlinelibrary.wiley.com/doi/abs/10.1113/jphysiol.1977.sp012072

9. J. O. Holloszy, and E. F. Coyle. "Adaptations of skeletal muscle to endurance exercise and their metabolic consequences" *Scientific Society Publisher Alliance*. Available at:https://www.physiology.org/doi/abs/10.1152/jappl.1984.56.4.831

10. Metabolic Healing. "Electrolytes & The Adrenals" Available at:https://metabolichealing.com/electrolytes-the-adrenals/

11. SynchroLife. "Heal Your Adrenals With Himalayan Salt." Available at:https://besynchro.com/blogs/blog/7149480-heal-your-adrenals-with-himalayan-salt

12. Meeusen R, Duclos M, Foster C, Fry A, Gleeson M, Nieman D, Raglin J, Rietjens G, Steinacker J, Urhausen A; European College of Sport Science; American College of Sports Medicine. "Prevention, diagnosis, and treatment of the overtraining syndrome: joint consensus statement of the European College of Sport Science and the American College of Sports Medicine." *Med Sci Sports Exerc. 2013 Jan;45(1):186-205*. Available at: https://www.ncbi.nlm.nih.gov/pubmed/23247672

13. DiNicolantonio JJ, Lucan SC, O' KeefeJH. "The Evidence for Saturated Fat and for Sugar Related to Coronary Heart Disease." *Prog Cardiovasc Dis. 2016 Mar-Apr;58(5):464-72* Available at: https://www.ncbi.nlm.nih.gov/pubmed/26586275

14. Rada P, Avena NM, Hoebel BG. "Daily bingeing on sugar repeatedly releases dopamine in the accumbens shell." *Neuroscience. 2005;134(3):737-44*. Available at:https://www.ncbi.nlm.nih.gov/pubmed/15987666

15. Colantuoni C, Rada P, McCarthy J, Patten C, Avena NM, Chadeayne A, Hoebel BG. "Evidence that intermittent, excessive sugar intake causes endogenous opioid dependence." *Obes Res. 2002 Jun;10(6):478-88*

16. American Heart Association. "Added Sugars Add to Your Risk of Dying from Heart Disease." Available at: http://www.heart.org/HEARTORG/ HealthyLiving/HealthyEating/Nutrition/Added-Sugars-Add-to-Your-Risk- of-Dying-from-Heart-Disease_UCM_460319_Article.jsp#.Wso6LmaZPOS

17. University of Tasmania. "New research reveals that 'taking a break from your diet' may improve weight loss." Available at: http://www.utas.edu.au/ latest-news/utas-homepage-news/new-research-reveals-that-taking-a- break-from-your-diet-may-improve-weight-loss

18. Dirlewanger M, di Vetta V, Guenat E, Battilana P, Seematter G, Schneiter P, Jéquier E, Tappy L. "Effects of short-term carbohydrate or fat overfeeding on energy expenditure and plasma leptin concentrations in healthy female subjects." *Int J Obes Relat Metab Disord. 2000 Nov;24(11):1413-8.*

19. Bigrigg JK, Heigenhauser GJ, Inglis JG, LeBlanc PJ, Peters SJ. "Carbohydrate refeeding after a high-fat diet rapidly reverses the adaptive increase in human skeletal muscle PDH kinase activity." *Am J Physiol Regul Integr Comp Physiol. 2009 Sep;297(3):R885-91.*

20. Thomas DeLauer December 2017. "What to Eat Before/After Cheat Meals" [Online Video] Available at: https://www.youtube.com/watch? v=zjS8MY78i_I

21. Reger MA, Henderson ST, Hale C, Cholerton B, Baker LD, Watson GS, Hyde K, Chapman D, Craft S. "Effects of beta-hydroxybutyrate on cognition in memory-impaired adults." *Neurobiol Aging. 2004 Mar;25(3):311-4.*

22. Longo VD, "Fasting: Molecular Mechanisms and Clinical Applications." *Cell Metabolism. Volume 19, Issue 2, p181–192, 4 February 2014.* Available at: http://www.cell.com/cell-metabolism/fulltext/S1550-4131(13)00503-2

23. K Y Ho, J D Veldhuis, M L Johnson, R Furlanetto, W S Evans, K G Alberti, and M O Thorner "Fasting enhances growth hormone secretion and amplifies the complex rhythms of growth hormone secretion in man." *J Clin Invest. 1988 Apr; 81(4): 968–975.*

24. Patterson RE, Sears DD "Metabolic Effects of Intermittent Fasting." *Annu Rev Nutr. 2017 Aug 21;37:371-393. doi: 10.1146/annurev-nutr-071816-064634.* Available at: https://www.ncbi.nlm.nih.gov/pubmed/28715993

25. Varady KA, Bhutani S, Church EC, Klempel MC. "Short-term modified alternate-day fasting: a novel dietary strategy for weight loss and cardioprotection in obese adults." *Am J Clin Nutr 2009; 90: 1138–1143.*

26. Berkhan M. "Intermittent Fasting For Weight Loss Preserves Muscle Mass?" Available at https://leangains.com/intermittent-fasting-for-weight-loss-preserves-muscle-mass/

27. Longo VD, Panda S, "Fasting, Circadian Rhythms, and Time-Restricted Feeding in Healthy Lifespan." *Cell Metab. 2016 Jun 14;23(6):1048-1059.* Available at https://www.ncbi.nlm.nih.gov/pubmed/27810402.

28. Raben A, Astrup A. "Manipulating carbohydrate content and sources in obesity prone subjects: effect on energy expenditure and macronutrient balance" *Int J Obes Relat Metab Disord. 1996 Mar.*

29. Eric T Trexler, Abbie E Smith-Ryan, and Layne E Norton, "Metabolic adaptation to weight loss: implications for the athlete." *J Int Soc Sports Nutr. 2014; 11: 7.* Available at: https://www.ncbi.nlm.nih.gov/pmc/articles/PMC3943438/

30. Lê KA, D'Alessio DA, Tappy L. "Metabolic effects of excess energy intake: does food composition matter?" *Curr Opin Clin Nutr Metab Care. 2010 Jul;13(4):429-31.* Available at: https://www.ncbi.nlm.nih.gov/pubmed/20489607

31. Brainum J. "A sugar that burns fat?" *Applied metabolics.*

32. Eric C Westman Richard D Feinman John C Mavropoulos Mary C Vernon Jeff S Volek James A Wortman William S Yancy Stephen D Phinney "Low-carbohydrate nutrition and metabolism" *The American Journal of Clinical Nutrition*, Volume 86, Issue 2, 1 August 2007, Pages 276–284.

33. McDonald L, "The rapid fat loss handbook."

34. J Galgani, E Ravussin "Energy metabolism, fuel selection and body weight regulation." *Int J Obes (Lond). 2008 Dec; 32(Suppl 7): S109–S119.*

35. Anssi H Manninen, "Is a Calorie Really a Calorie? Metabolic Advantage of Low-Carbohydrate Diets." *J Int Soc Sports Nutr. 2004; 1(2): 21–26.* Available at: https://www.ncbi.nlm.nih.gov/pmc/articles/PMC2129158/

36. Hopkins M, Blundell JE "Energy balance, body composition, sedentariness and appetite regulation: pathways to obesity" *Clin Sci (Lond). 2016 Sep 1;130(18):1615-28.* Available at: https://www.ncbi.nlm.nih.gov/pubmed/27503946?dopt=Abstract

37. Legge A et al "How to Set a Caloric Deficit for Fat Loss." Available at: https://completehumanperformance.com/2013/10/15/fat-loss-deficit/

38. Catherine M. Champagne, PhD, RD, LDN, FADA, Professor-Research, Stephanie T Broyles, PhD, Assistant Professor, Laura D. Moran, MS, RD, LDN, Clinical Dietitian, Katherine C. Cash, RD, LDN, Research Dietitian/Interventionist, Erma J. Levy, MPH, RD, Research Dietitian/Interventionist, Pao-Hwa Lin, PhD, Associate Research Professor, Bryan C. Batch, MD, Lillian F. Lien, MD, Medical Director, Duke Inpatient Diabetes Management, Assistant Professor, Department of Medicine, Kristine L. Funk, MS, RD, Research Associate III, Arlene Dalcin, RD, LDN, Research Associate, Catherine Loria, PhD, MS, MA, FAHA, Nutritional Epidemiologist, and Valerie H. Myers, PhD, Instructor, Behavioral Medicine "Dietary intakes associated with successful weight loss and maintenance during the Weight Loss Maintenance Trial." *J Am Diet Assoc. 2011 Dec; 111(12): 1826–1835*. Available at: https://www.ncbi.nlm.nih.gov/pmc/articles/ PMC3225890/

39. J C K Wells, M S Fewtrell "Measuring body composition." *Arch Dis Child. 2006 Jul; 91(7): 612–617*. Available at: https://www.ncbi.nlm.nih.gov/pmc/articles/ PMC2082845/

40. Dana L. Duren, Ph.D, Richard J. Sherwood, Ph.D, Stefan A. Czerwinski, Ph.D.,1 Miryoung Lee, Ph.D, Audrey C. Choh, Ph.D, Roger M. Siervogel, Ph.D, and Wm. Cameron Chumlea, Ph.D, "Body Composition Methods: Comparisons and Interpretation." *J Diabetes Sci Technol. 2008 Nov; 2(6): 1139–1146*. Available at: https://www.ncbi.nlm.nih.gov/pmc/articles/PMC2769821/

41. JDeNovo July 2012. "How to count macros" [Online Video] Available at:https:// www.youtube.com/watch? v=YUh3tmfM35w&desktop_uri=%2Fwatch%3Fv%3DYUh3tmfM35w&app=des ktop

42. McDonald L. "Macronutrient Intake for Mass Gains." Available at: https://bodyrecomposition.com/muscle-gain/macronutrient-intake-for-mass-gains-qa.html/

43. Samantha M. Solon-Biet, Aisling C. McMahon, J. William O. Ballard, Kari Ruohonen, Lindsay E. Wu, Victoria C. Cogger, Alessandra Warren, Xin Huang, Nicolas Pichaud, Richard G. Melvin, Rahul Gokarn, Mamdouh Khalil, Nigel Turner, Gregory J. Cooney, David A. Sinclair, David Raubenheimer, David G. Le Couteur, and Stephen J. Simpson. "The Ratio of Macronutrients, Not Caloric Intake, Dictates Cardiometabolic Health, Ageing, and Longevity in Ad Libitum-Fed Mice." *Cell Metab. 2014 Mar 4; 19(3): 418–430.*

44. Frank M. Sacks, M.D, George A. Bray, M.D, Vincent J. Carey, Ph.D, Steven R. Smith, M.D, Donna H. Ryan, M.D, Stephen D. Anton, Ph.D, Katherine McManus, M.S., R.D, Catherine M. Champagne, Ph.D, Louise M. Bishop, M.S., R.D, Nancy Laranjo, B.A, Meryl S. Leboff, M.D, Jennifer C. Rood, Ph.D, Lilian de Jonge, Ph.D, Frank L. Greenway, M.D, Catherine M. Loria, Ph.D, Eva Obarzanek, Ph.D, and Donald A. Williamson, Ph.D. "Comparison of Weight-Loss Diets with Different Compositions of Fat, Protein, and Carbohydrates" *N Engl J Med. 2009 Feb 26; 360(9): 859–873.*

45. Lambert CP, Frank LL, Evans WJ. "Macronutrient considerations for the sport of bodybuilding." *Sports Med. 2004;34(5):317-27.*

46. Venn BJ, Green TJ. "Glycemic index and glycemic load: measurement issues and their effect on diet-disease relationships." *Eur J Clin Nutr. 2007 Dec;61 Suppl 1:S122-31.* Available at: https://www.ncbi.nlm.nih.gov/pubmed/17992183

47. Brand-Miller J, Buyken AE. "The glycemic index issue." Curr Opin Lipidol. 2012 Feb;23(1):62-7. Available at: https://www.ncbi.nlm.nih.gov/pubmed/22157060

48. Mayo Clinic. "Nutrition and healthy eating." Available at: https://www.mayoclinic.org/healthy-lifestyle/nutrition-and-healthy-eating/in-depth/fiber/art-20043983

49. Agnes N. Pedersen, Jens Kondrup, and Elisabet Børsheim "Health effects of protein intake in healthy adults: a systematic literature review." *Food Nutr Res. 2013; 57: 10.3402.* Available at: https://www.ncbi.nlm.nih.gov/pmc/articles/PMC3730112/

50. Eric R Helms, Alan A Aragon, and Peter J Fitschen. "Evidence-based recommendations for natural bodybuilding contest preparation: nutrition and supplementation." *J Int Soc Sports Nutr. 2014; 11: 20.* Available at: https://www.ncbi.nlm.nih.gov/pmc/articles/PMC4033492/

51. Tomiyama,A, et al. "Low calorie dieting increases cortisol." *Pschocom Med 2007;72:357-64.*

52. McDonald L. "Applied Nutrition for Mixed Sports." *Bodyrecomposition (2010).*

53. Knuth, ND, et al. "Metabolic adaptation following massive weight loss is related to the degree of energy imbalance and changes in circulating leptin." *Obesity 2014;22:2563-2569.*

54. Calbet, J, et al. "A time-efficient reduction of fat mass in 4 days with exercise and caloric restriction." *Scand J Sci Med Sports 2014.*

55. Davoodi, S, et al. "Calorie shifting versus calorie restriction diet: A comparative clinical trial." *Int J Prevent Med 2014;5: 447-56.*

56. *Wing* R R, Phelan S, "Long-term weight loss maintenance." *The American Journal of Clinical Nutrition*, Volume 82, Issue 1, 1 July 2005, Pages 222S–225S. Available at: https://doi.org/10.1093/ajcn/82.1.222S

57. Davoodi, S, et al. "Calorie shifting versus calorie restriction diet: A comparative clinical trial." *Int J Prevent Med 2014;5: 447-56.*

58. *Wing* R R, Phelan S, "Long-term weight loss maintenance." *The American Journal of Clinical Nutrition*, Volume 82, Issue 1, 1 July 2005, Pages 222S–225S. Available at: https://doi.org/10.1093/ajcn/82.1.222S

59. Gibala, M, et al. Metabolic adaptations to short-term high-intensity interval training: A little pain for a lot of gain? Exercise and Sports Sci Rev 2008;36:58-63. Available at: https://www.ncbi.nlm.nih.gov/pubmed/18362686

60. Copeland SR, Mills MC, Lerner JL, Crizer MF, Thompson CW, Sullivan JM, "Haemodynamic effects of aerobic vs resistance training." Available at: https://www.ncbi.nlm.nih.gov/pubmed/9004105

61. Whyte, LJ, et al. Effects of a single bout of very high-intensity exercise of metabolic health in overweight/obese sedentary men. Metabolism 2012.

62. Boutcher, SH. High-intensity intermittent exercise and fat loss.J obesity 2011.

63. Wolpert, S. "Dieting does not work, UCLA researcher's report." *Journal of American Psychological Association.*

64. Frank M. Sacks, George A. Bray, Vincent J. Carey, Steven R Smith, Donna H. Ryan, Stephen D. Anton, Katherine McManus, Catherine M. Champagne, Louise M. Bishop, Nancy Laranjo, Meryl S. Leboff, Jennifer C. Rood, Lilian de Jonge, Frank L. Greenway, Catherine M. Loria, Eva Obarzanek, and Donald A. Williamson, "Comparison of Weight-Loss Diets with Different Compositions of Fat, Protein, and Carbohydrates," *New England Journal of Medicine 360 (Feb 26, 2009): 859-73.*

65. Noakes M, Foster PR, Keogh JB, James AP, Mamo JC, Clifton PM, "Comparison of isocaloric very low carbohydrate/high saturated fat and high carbohydrate/low saturated fat diets on body composition and cardiovascular risk." *Nutr Metab (Lond). 2006 Jan 11;3:7.*

66. Surwit RS, Feinglos MN, McCaskill CC, Clay SL, Babyak MA, Brownlow BS, Plaisted CS, Lin PH, "Metabolic and behavioural effects of a high-sucrose diet during weight loss." *Am J Clin Nutr. 1997 Apr; 65(4):908-15.*

67. Strasser B, Spreitzer A, Haber P, "Fat loss depends on energy deficit only, independently of the method for weight loss." *Ann Nutr Metab. 2007;51(5):428-32. Epub 2007 Nov 20.*

68. Buchholz AC, Schoeller DA, "Is a calorie a calorie?" *Am J Clin Nutr. Volume 79, Issue 5, 1 May 2004, Pages 899S-906S,* http://doi.org/10.1093/ajcn/79.5.899S.

69. Guyenet S, "The carbohydrate hypothesis of obesity: a Critical Examination" *Nutrition and Health Science.* Available at: http://wholehealthsource.blogspot.co.uk/2011/08/carbohydrate-hypothesis-of-obesity.html

70. Golay A, Allaz AF, Ybarra J, Bianchi P, Saraiva S, Mensi N, Gomis R, de Tonnac N. "Similar weight loss with low-energy food combining or balanced diets." *Int J Obes Relat Metab Disord. 2000 Apr;24(4):492-6,* https://www.ncbi.nlm.nih.gov/pubmed/10805507.

71. Joosen AMCP, Westerterp KR. "Energy expenditure during overfeeding." *Nutr Metab (Lond). 2006;3:25.* doi:10.1186/1743-7075-3-25.

72. Horton TJ, Drougas H, Brachey A, Reed GW, Peters JC, Hill JO. "Fat and carbohydrate overfeeding in humans: different effects on energy storage." *Am J Clin Nutr*. 1995;62(1):19–29. Available at: https://ajcn.nutrition.org/content/62/1/19.long.

73. Nordqvist C, "Nutrition professor loses 27 pounds on junk food diet in 10 weeks" *Medical News Today (November 2010). Available at:* https://www.medicalnewstoday.com/articles/207071.php

74. Pawlowski A, "Man loses nearly 40 lbs. eating only McDonald's" *Medical News Today (October 2016). Available at:* https://www.today.com/health/man-loses-nearly-40-lbs-eating-only-mcdonalds-2D11863528

75. Guyenet S, "Interview with Chris Voigt of 20 Potatoes a Day" *Nutrition and Health Science*. Available at: http://wholehealthsource.blogspot.co.uk/2010/12/interview-with-chris-voigt-of-20.html

BOOKS

1. Aragon A. (2007) Girth Control: The Science of Fat Loss and Muscle Gain, 1st Edition.

2. Lee J. (2019) "The Ultimate Gym Workout."

3. Lee J. (2018) "The Essential Guide to Sports Nutrition and Bodybuilding."

4. Lee J. (2018) "Lean Gains (2nd edition)"

PICTURES

1. https://www.shutterstock.com/image-photo/boy-chef-prepares-rice-vegetables-498832138

2. https://www.shutterstock.com/image-photo/muscular-man-doing-exercises-dumbbells-biceps-588411014

3. https://www.shutterstock.com/image-photo/full-length-rear-view-shot-two-1040808109

4. https://www.shutterstock.com/image-photo/beautiful-young-woman-measuring-tape-isolated-116440234

5. https://www.shutterstock.com/image-photo/sexy-athletic-girl-working-out-gym-1174499368

6. https://www.shutterstock.com/image-photo/strong-woman-workout-medicine-ball-photo-1140913235

7. https://www.shutterstock.com/image-photo/athletic-slim-woman-measuring-her-waist-222406171

8. https://www.shutterstock.com/image-photo/female-sculptor-creates-beautiful-body-sporty-1126182893

9. https://www.shutterstock.com/image-photo/pretty-young-woman-wearing-boxing-gloves-177198008

10. https://www.shutterstock.com/image-photo/fit-young-woman-fighting-off-sweets-1145417207

11. https://www.shutterstock.com/image-photo/clever-confident-female-student-classroom-writing-157640708

12. https://www.shutterstock.com/image-photo/smiling-girl-sportswear-holding-glass-bowl-488900869

13. https://www.shutterstock.com/image-photo/beautiful-young-sporty-couple-posing-showing-203201410

14. https://www.shutterstock.com/image-vector/beautiful-realistic-fitness-vector-front-view-1285419733

15. https://www.shutterstock.com/image-photo/two-black-metal-dumbbells-on-isolated-621179231

16. https://www.shutterstock.com/image-photo/barbell-isolated-on-white-background-1139066726

17. https://www.shutterstock.com/image-photo/group-weights-on-white-background-394401289

18. https://www.shutterstock.com/image-photo/young-male-athlete-holding-bottle-protein-329808695

19. https://www.shutterstock.com/image-photo/collage-woman-body-before-after-weight-1095041834

20. https://www.shutterstock.com/image-photo/fitness-woman-doing-jump-step-ups-1155383425

21. https://www.shutterstock.com/image-photo/sports-guy-sexy-girl-posing-studio-477042676

22. https://www.shutterstock.com/image-photo/womans-body-before-after-weight-loss-758468800

23. https://www.shutterstock.com/image-photo/fit-man-pointing-front-over-white-167332247

24. https://www.shutterstock.com/image-photo/muscular-shirtless-black-male-bodybuilder-drinking-1136212946

25. https://www.shutterstock.com/image-photo/beautiful-sporty-muscular-woman-working-out-338402264

26. https://www.shutterstock.com/image-photo/black-bodybuilder-training-dumbbells-strong-man-149726210

27. https://www.shutterstock.com/image-photo/black-bodybuilder-topless-showing-his-muscles-151404668

28. https://www.shutterstock.com/image-photo/fit-young-woman-holding-healthy-green-786227692

29. https://www.shutterstock.com/image-photo/fit-man-woman-stretching-legs-on-256322692

30. https://www.shutterstock.com/image-photo/resting-time-sporty-girl-bottle-water-281327639

31. https://www.shutterstock.com/image-photo/muscular-male-doing-crossfit-training-749638846

32. https://www.shutterstock.com/image-photo/fitness-model-exercising-dumbbells-both-hands-640663678

33. https://www.shutterstock.com/image-photo/portrait-sporty-young-couple-arms-crossed-180186092

34. https://www.shutterstock.com/image-photo/cropped-conceptual-inspiration-lifestyle-photo-female-1032601543

35. https://www.shutterstock.com/image-photo/beautiful-woman-holding-cheeseburger-saying-no-615731183

36. https://www.shutterstock.com/image-photo/handsome-teen-boy-black-tshirt-making-1355869112

37. https://www.shutterstock.com/image-photo/strong-athletic-man-showing-muscular-body-330847334

38. https://www.shutterstock.com/image-photo/woman-on-stationary-bike-overtraining-symptoms-609599879

39. https://www.shutterstock.com/image-photo/sporty-woman-doing-boxing-exercises-making-1008118453

40. https://www.shutterstock.com/image-photo/before-after-result-group-three-young-688201441

41. https://www.shutterstock.com/image-photo/smiling-sports-woman-standing-arms-folded-534983347

42. https://www.shutterstock.com/image-photo/fit-woman-stretching-her-leg-warm-107519378

43. https://www.shutterstock.com/image-photo/charming-young-millennial-model-pink-dyed-1077151898

44. https://www.shutterstock.com/image-photo/woman-doing-exercises-abdominal-muscles-isolated-85094836

45. https://www.shutterstock.com/image-photo/muscular-shirtless-black-male-bodybuilder-drinking-1136212946

46. https://www.shutterstock.com/image-photo/young-cheerful-couple-jogging-over-white-135662486

47. https://www.shutterstock.com/image-photo/attractive-athletic-girl-showing-biceps-269789696

Printed in Great Britain
by Amazon